FLOORED! SUPERCARS

McLAREN

By Jared Gall

45TH PARALLEL PRESS

Published in the United States of America by Cherry Lake Publishing Group
Ann Arbor, Michigan
www.cherrylakepublishing.com

Reading Adviser: Beth Walker Gambro, MS, Ed., Reading Consultant, Yorkville, IL

Photo Credits: © Brandon Woyshnis/Shutterstock, cover, title page; © Qadir Aras/Shutterstock, 3; © Brandon Woyshnis/Shutterstock, 4, 6–7; Eric Koch for Anefo, CC0, via Wikimedia Commons, 8; © Sean.zen/Shutterstock, 10; Eric Koch for Anefo / neg. stroken, 1945-1989, 2.24.01.05, item number 919-3824, CC BY-SA 3.0 NL via Wikimedia Commons, 11; I, Pyrope, CC BY-SA 3.0 via Wikimedia Commons, 12; © Dan74/Shutterstock, 13; © Ev. Safronov/Shutterstock, 14; © dimcars/Shutterstock, 16; © Gurpreet Mann/iStock, 18; © Johnnie Rik/Shutterstock, 19; © Jens Mommens/Shutterstock, 20; Ron Kimball/KimballStock, 22–23; © Brandon Woyshnis/iStock.com, 24; © Sport car hub/Shutterstock, 26, 28–29; Mike Cookson, CC BY-SA 4.0 via Wikimedia Commons, 30 (top); © Maurie Hill/Dreamstime.com, 30 (bottom); © Brandon Woyshnis/Shutterstock, 31 (top); © Tim Wilkens/Shutterstock, 31 (bottom)

45th Parallel Press is an imprint of Cherry Lake Publishing Group.

Library of Congress Cataloging-in-Publication Data

Names: Gall, Jared, author.
Title: McLaren / by Jared Gall.
Description: Ann Arbor, Michigan : 45th Parallel Press, [2025] | Series: Floored! Supercars | Audience: Grades 4-6 | Summary: "Tech and innovation are at the forefront of luxury supercars. This book explores the cool features that make McLarens some of the best high-performance vehicles in the world. From the history of the brand, to fast facts, and awesome photos--these books have enough to keep any car enthusiast engaged. This high-interest series is written at a low readability to aid struggling readers. Books feature educational sidebars, table of contents, glossary, index, author biography, and timeline"-- Provided by publisher.
Identifiers: LCCN 2024035952 | ISBN 9781668956632 (hardcover) | ISBN 9781668957486 (paperback) | ISBN 9781668958353 (ebook) | ISBN 9781668959220 (pdf)
Subjects: LCSH: McLaren automobiles--History--Juvenile literature. | McLaren automobiles--Design and construction--Juvenile literature.
Classification: LCC TL236.15.M35 G35 2025 | DDC 629.222/2--dc23/eng/20240923
LC record available at https://lccn.loc.gov/2024035952

Printed in the United States of America

Note from Publisher: Websites change regularly, and their future contents are outside of our control. Supervise children when conducting any recommended online searches for extended learning opportunities.

ABOUT THE AUTHOR:

Jared Gall writes about cars and trucks for magazines and websites. He has driven everything from semitrucks and school buses to sports cars and supercars. He has raced off-road buggies through the desert in Mexico and Mercedes-Benzes on frozen lakes in Sweden. He has driven a lot of Mercedes-Benzes, but never an AMG One. His personal top speed is 189 miles (304.2 kilometers) per hour, set while driving a Ferrari.

Table of Contents

McLaren doesn't make SUVs. It makes only supercars.

CHAPTER 1

Introduction

There are many kinds of cars. They're good at different things. Minivans have lots of space. Whole families can fit. They can ride together to school. They can ride together on vacation. **Sport utility vehicles** are called SUVs. They also have lots of space. They're made to tow heavy things. They tow boats. They tow campers. They also go off-roading.

Sports cars are built to be fast. They're fun to drive. They're small. They're light. This makes them **agile**. Agile means they can turn quickly and easily. They go around corners fast.

Supercars are like sports cars. But they go even faster. Their engines have more power. They're lighter. They go faster on straight roads. They turn faster. Many are built with special metal. This makes them extra light.

Most supercars sit low. They're close to the ground. This makes them **aerodynamic**. That means they move through air easily. Imagine putting your hand out a car window. Imagine facing your palm into the wind. It would be hard to keep your hand still. But what if you lay your hand flat? It would then be easier to hold your hand steady. Your hand is more aerodynamic

when it's flat. Being aerodynamic makes supercars fast.

Have you ever seen a McLaren? Have you seen one on the road? If so, then you have seen a supercar! McLarens are special. Let's learn more.

McLarens are unique. They have a high status. They're dream cars. They impress people.

Bruce McLaren won 4 grand prix races. Since 1959, McLaren Racing has won 184 more grand prix races.

CHAPTER 2

McLaren History

Bruce McLaren founded the McLaren company. He was born in 1937 in New Zealand. His parents owned a car repair shop. His dad liked to race cars. So did he. He was a good race car driver. But New Zealand is a small country. It's an island. It's in the ocean. It's near Australia. It's far from everywhere else. There aren't many jobs for race car drivers.

McLaren moved to Europe. He did this in 1958. Racing is very popular in Europe. McLaren started winning races right away. In 1959, he won his first **grand prix**. A grand prix is a race. It's what **Formula 1**, or F1, races are called. Formula 1 race cars are the world's fastest race cars. McLaren was the youngest person to win this race.

McLaren kept winning races. He started working on his own race cars. He made them faster. At first, he **modified** cars built by others. Modify means to change and improve. McLaren built his first race car in 1964. His car was so fast. Other people wanted it. He built more. Other race car drivers bought them. McLaren became a car company.

McLaren made his first logo. The logo has a picture of a race car. It also has a picture of a kiwi. A **kiwi** is a New Zealand bird. Kiwi is also a nickname for people from New Zealand. Later, McLaren changed the logo. The new logo looked like a **checkered** flag. Checkered is a pattern of squares. The squares alternate colors. A checkered flag is used in races. It's waved at the end. It means victory. Today, the logo is just a single shape. The shape is rounded. This makes it look like it's moving fast.

New Zealand Kiwi

Bruce McLaren died at the young age of 32. He won 22 races during his short career, from 1959 to 1969.

The McLaren company started in 1963. The first car was the McLaren M1A.

McLaren was busy building race cars. But he didn't stop racing. He won the **24 Hours of Le Mans**.

The 24 Hours of Le Mans is a famous race. It's in France. It happens once every year. It lasts 24 hours straight. That's a whole day and night! It starts on a Saturday afternoon. It ends the next afternoon. Teams of drivers take turns driving. They take turns eating. They take turns sleeping. The winner finishes the most laps in 24 hours. McLaren won it in 1966. He was driving a Ford GT40.

The **Can-Am racing series** started in 1966. It takes place in Canada (Can) and America (Am). That's why it's called Can-Am. Can-Am race cars were faster than Formula 1 cars.

Can-Am racing made McLaren cars famous. The Can-Am series lasted 9 years. McLaren cars won more than half of Can-Am races. Between 1967 and 1971, they won almost every race. They won 37 out of 43 races.

McLaren race cars were also winning Formula 1 races. They won more races. They won the **Indy 500**. The Indy 500 is a famous race in the United States. McLaren was now a famous name.

For several years, Can-Am cars were the world's fastest race cars.

Amelia Lewis helped make McLaren F1 cars lighter. She still works with the team to make their cars better!

Behind the Wheel

Amelia Lewis grew up watching racing. She watched Formula 1. She watched with her dad. There aren't many women in F1. Lewis never thought she'd be one of them. The McLaren company inspired her. She said, "It was only when McLaren gave a talk at my university that I realized working for a racing team wasn't a dream. It was something I really could do."

Lewis is an **engineer**. Engineers design things. They build things. Lewis applied for a job with Williams. Williams is another F1 team. She got the job. After working for Williams, she got a new job. She worked with the McLaren F1 team. To be fast, race cars need to be lightweight. Lewis's first job at McLaren was to make cars lighter. She now works with the drivers. She figures out how to improve cars.

The McLaren F1 supercar went from 0 to 60 miles (0 to 96.6 kilometers) per hour in 3.2 seconds.

CHAPTER 3

McLaren Evolution

McLaren cars were winning races all over the world. McLaren decided to build a supercar. Supercars are different from race cars. And race cars are different from everyday road cars. They have to go fast. But road cars need to be more. They need to be comfortable. They need to be safe. They need to have room for people and things.

McLaren's new car came out in 1992. The company named the supercar after Formula 1 racing. It called it the F1. It wanted the F1 to be the fastest supercar ever.

The F1 is a **mid-engine**. That means the engine is behind the driver. It's in the middle of the car. This makes cars more aerodynamic. In normal cars, the engine is in front of the driver. Most supercars are mid-engines. The McLaren F1 was made out of **carbon fiber**. Carbon fiber is very light. It's very strong. It's also very costly. The McLaren F1 cost $1 million. A normal car cost about $20,000 at the time. But the F1 was very special. It was the world's fastest car.

The Lamborghini Diablo is another famous supercar. It was built in 1992. It came out at the same time as the F1. The Diablo could go 204 miles (328.3 km) per hour. That's very fast. The

Only 106 McLaren F1s were made. It is a rare car.

McLarens have metal grills on the back. This keeps the exhaust pipes free of debris.

McLaren F1 was faster. It could go 241 miles (387.9 km) per hour. It was more than 20 years before a faster car came out.

McLaren built only 106 F1s. The company had built it to drive on the streets. But it was so fast. People wanted to race it. McLaren then modified the F1. The company took it to the 24 Hours of Le Mans. This happened in 1995.

The 24 Hours of Le Mans lasts 24 hours straight. That's a whole day and night! It starts on a Saturday afternoon. It ends on a Sunday Afternoon. It took place on June 17 and 18 in 1995. It rained that year. It rained for 17 of the 24 hours!

The first 24 Hours of Le Mans race only had 33 cars. In 2024, there were 62 cars.

The Le Mans race track is 8.5 miles (13.7 km) long. That's 2 times longer than an F1 racetrack. It's 3 times longer than a **NASCAR** track. NASCAR stands for the National Association for **Stock Car** Auto Racing. A stock car is a car that hasn't been changed. Nothing is added to or taken from the car. Most of the Le Mans track is public roads. These roads are closed only for the race. In 24 hours, the winning F1 drove 2,520 miles (4,055.5 km). That's like driving across the United States!

Fast Facts

- McLaren was the first to build a race car out of carbon fiber. It did this in 1981. Today, most race cars are made from carbon fiber.
- 1988 was McLaren's best year in Formula 1 history. It won 15 out of 16 races.
- McLaren won 43 of the 71 Can-Am races. It did this over 10 years.
- McLaren raced in the Indy 500. It did this 6 times. It won 3 times. It finished in second place twice.
- McLaren's race cars were popular. It couldn't build enough of them. It had to hire another company to build the cars.
- Most teams in Formula 1 racing don't build their own engines. McLaren uses Mercedes-Benz engines.

The McLaren F1 was faster than other supercars. But it wasn't meant to be a race car. It was 90 percent road car. Many didn't think it would win. The race was exciting. J. J. Lehto is a Finnish racing driver. He was one of the F1 drivers at Le Mans. He drove the car at night. He did this in the rain. His driving gave McLaren an edge.

McLaren won the race. It did this on its first try. McLaren F1s also finished in third, fourth, and fifth places. A supercar beat all of the race cars. That has never happened again.

McLaren stopped making the F1 in 1998. The company kept racing. But it didn't build another supercar for almost 15 years.

MP4-12C is also called the McLaren 12C. It was built in secret.

CHAPTER 4

McLaren Today

McLaren started building supercars again. This happened in 2012. It has been building them ever since. Race cars don't have names like road cars do. They have numbers. The numbers are like code names. McLaren gave its next supercar a code name. It called it the MP4-12C.

The MP4-12C had a turbocharged engine. Turbocharged means it has a **turbocharger**. A turbocharger is a small fan. It blows air into the engine. This helps the engine make more power. Today, McLaren's supercars all have turbochargers.

In 2013, McLaren built its first **hybrid**. Hybrid cars have a gas engine and an electric motor. They're more **efficient** than regular cars. Efficient means not wasting energy. Efficient cars can drive farther on less gas.

McLaren named their hybrid the **P1**. In Formula 1 racing, P1 means "Place One." It means first place. The P1 was very, very fast. McLaren built only 375 P1s.

McLaren also made an even faster version. This one was called the P1 GTR. The P1 GTR isn't **street legal**. That means it's too fast for public roads. P1 GTR owners can drive it only on racetracks.

The McLaren P1 has a computer system that only allows it to go up to 217 miles (349.2km) per hour.

Cost of Ownership

MODEL	PRICE
2024 Toyota Camry	$27,500
2024 Honda CR-V	$31,000
2024 Ford F-150	$39,000

MODEL	PRICE
2024 McLaren GTS	$209,000
2024 McLaren Artura	$233,000
2024 McLaren 750S	$305,000
2019 McLaren Elva	$1,675,000
2020 McLaren Speedtail	$2,100,000
2023 McLaren Solus GT	$4,000,000

Porsche and Ferrari are other companies. They make supercars. They also make hybrid supercars. Their hybrids also came out in 2013. They also built only a small number. Each one cost about $1 million. Today, people call these 3 cars the **holy trinity**. This means they're the top 3 hybrid supercars.

In 2023, another McLaren hybrid supercar came out. It's called the Artura. Unlike the P1, McLaren is not limiting the number of Arturas. Anyone can buy one. But they must have enough money. The Artura is cheaper than a P1. But it's still expensive. It costs $233,000.

The McLaren Speedtail has top-notch aerodynamics. This helps it go faster than any other McLaren before.

When the F1 came out, it was the only car McLaren made. Today, it makes many more cars. It still makes the Artura. It also sells the 750S and GTS. And it makes extra-special supercars like the P1. But it builds only a few of those.

One extra-special McLaren is called the Speedtail. It looks like the F1. It's a hybrid. It's way more powerful than the F1. It can go 250 miles (402.3 km) per hour. That's faster than some airplanes fly. The Speedtail is the fastest McLaren ever. At least, it's the fastest McLaren so far. Do you think the company will make a faster car in the future?

Timeline of a Legend

1937

Bruce McLaren is born.

1959

McLaren wins his first Formula 1 Grand Prix at age 22. He becomes the youngest winner.

1964

McLaren builds his first race car. The car is called the M1A.

1965

McLaren build his first Formula 1 ca

1966

McLaren wins the 2 Hours of Le Mans. H drives a Ford GT40.

1968

A McLaren car wins its first Formula 1 race. McLaren is the driver.

1970

Bruce McLaren is killed in a car crash while testing the McLaren M8D. He is 32 years old.

1972

McLaren wins its first Indy 500.

1995

McLaren starts making the McLaren F1. This is the company's first road car.

2012

MP4-12C is introduced. McLaren keeps making supercars.

Find Out More

BOOKS

Duling, Kaitlyn. *McLaren Elva.* Minneapolis, MN: Bellwether Media, 2024.

Murray, Julie. *McLaren F1.* Minneapolis, MN: Abdo Zoom, 2020.

WEBSITES

Search these online sources with an adult:

McLaren Facts for Kids | Kiddle

McLaren | Cool Kid Facts

Glossary

24 Hours of Le Mans (twen-tee-FOHR OW-uhrz uhv luh MAHNZ) a famous endurance race in France

aerodynamic (air-oh-dye-NAA-mik) able to move easily through the air

agile (A-juhl) able to change direction quickly

Can-Am racing series (CAN-AM RAY-sing SEE-reez) a series of car races that took place in Canada and America

carbon fiber (KAR-buhn FYE-buhr) a very strong, lightweight material

checkered (CHEH-kerd) covered with a pattern of squares

efficient (ih-FIH-shuhnt) able to be more productive with less energy

engineer (en-juh-NEER) a person who designs and builds things

Formula 1 (FOR-myuh-luh WUHN) a racing series with the fastest race cars in the world; also called F1

grand prix (gran-PREE) one of a series of international formula car races

holy trinity (HOH-lee TRIH-nuh-tee) a group of 3 things or people that are the most important in 1 area of interest

hybrid (HIYE-bruhd) a car with a gasoline engine and an electric motor

Indy 500 (IN-dee FYEV HUN-druhd) also known as the Indianapolis 500; one of the most famous annual car races in the United States

kiwi (KEE-wee) flightless New Zealand bird; a person from New Zealand

mid-engine (mid-EN-juhn) having the engine behind the driver

modified (MAH-duh-fiyed) changed or improved

NASCAR (NAS-kar) stands for National Association for Stock Car Auto Racing

P1 (PEE WUN) short for "place one" in Formula 1 racing; a very fast McLaren model

sport utility vehicles (SPORT yoo-TIH-luh-tee VEE-uh-kuhlz) vehicles designed to be used on rough surfaces but often used on city streets; also called SUVs

stock car (STAHK KAHR) a car used for racing that hasn't been modified from its original factory condition

street legal (STREET LEE-guhl) allowed to be driven on public roads

supercars (SOO-per-kahrz) cars designed to go faster than other cars

turbocharger (TER-boh-char-juhr) a small fan that blows air into the engine and produces more power

Index